ELY Cathedral
SOUVENIR GUIDE

PETER SILLS

Foundations

There has been a church in Ely since Christianity first came to England. 'When the Christian faith was in its infancy, a monastery had been built in Ely in honour of the ever-virgin Mary by blessed Augustine, apostle of the English.' So wrote one of the monks of Ely in the *Liber Eliensis*, a history of the Isle of Ely from the seventh to the twelfth centuries. Nothing more is known of this church, but the story continues about seventy years later with the desire of a Saxon princess to enter the religious life. Etheldreda was the daughter of Anna, King of the East Angles, and like her father, she became an ardent Christian.

Etheldreda's story is told in a series of eight sculptures on the Octagon pillars. She always felt called to the religious life, but for political reasons she was married first to Tonbert, leader of the people called the South Gyrwas, who gave her the land and royal rights to the Isle of Ely; and after his death, to Egfrid, heir to the kingdom of Northumbria. Her marriage to Egfrid was unhappy, and after twelve years she obtained his consent to retire to a convent to become a nun. Egfrid regretted his decision to let her go and set off in pursuit. But Etheldreda escaped him and after a hazardous journey arrived safely back in Ely where, in AD 673, she founded a double monastery for men and women. Etheldreda was Abbess for only seven years; she died of a tumour in the neck and was buried in a simple grave. Her sister, Seaxburga, who succeeded her, exhumed her body and moved it into the church.

Contemporary accounts relate that the body was incorrupt and that the tumour had been healed: 'Her linen clothes looked fresh as new, and touching them had the effect of casting out devils, and the wood of her coffin cured blindness.' Not surprisingly, Ethedreda was soon acknowledged as a saint and Ely became a place of pilgrimage, a tradition that has recently been revived with the annual St Etheldreda Pilgrimage on the Saturday nearest to 23 June, her Feast Day.

LEFT: A page from the *Liber Eliensis*.

OPPOSITE: The medieval wall painting in St Edmund's Chapel, showing his martyrdom at the hands of the Vikings in AD 870. Edmund was King of East Anglia; he refused to deny his Christian faith and was tied to a tree and shot through with arrows. This is one of the few medieval wall paintings to have survived at Ely.

ABOVE: Window over the West Door, showing St Etheldreda with her pastoral staff.

TOP RIGHT AND RIGHT: Two of the eight carvings in the Octagon, recording the life of St Etheldreda. *Above*, her marriage to Egfrid; *below*, resting on her flight from Northumberland to Ely.

The Benedictine Monastery

Etheldreda's church was destroyed by the Vikings when they invaded England in 869, and it languished in ruins until *c.*970, when the monastery was refounded. It became a Benedictine abbey for men only, and the monastic life was lived in Ely under the Rule of St Benedict for 570 years until the Dissolution of the Monasteries in 1539. The Chapel of St Dunstan and St Ethelwold in the South Transept commemorates the two saints who were responsible for the restoration of the monastery: Dunstan, Archbishop of Canterbury from 960 to 988, and his friend Ethelwold, Bishop of Winchester from 963 to 984. As Abbot of Glastonbury, Dunstan had been responsible for restoring the monastic life of England, which had all but died out following the Viking invasion. Under the protection of King Edgar, he reformed the English Church, ushering in a 'Golden Age'. It has been said that the tenth century gave shape to English history, and that Dunstan gave shape to the tenth century. As with other Benedictine abbeys, Ely was an important instrument in shaping the Christian identity and culture of Europe.

The beginning of the second millennium brought great upheaval for the Abbey. The fen people, led by Hereward 'the Wake', were the last to hold out against the Normans, but in 1070 they surrendered to the conquerors. King William installed Simeon, the Prior of Winchester, as Abbot, and, at the age of eighty-seven, he set about rebuilding the whole church. Bringing limestone from Barnack near Stamford, by water across the

Fens, the Norman master builders created a majestic church with its soaring pillars and round arches. With its uninterrupted view from west to east, the Nave of Ely is one of the most inspiring interiors in England. In size and beauty it proclaimed the glory of God; it also reflected the power of the Norman conquerors and the wealth and prestige of the monastic community.

ABOVE: The South Transept, part of the earliest surviving Norman work in the Cathedral. The arcade at the south end was added during the 12th century and the upper window formed when the new ceiling was constructed in the 14th century.

OPPOSITE: Ely's magnificent Nave - one of the longest of any UK Cathedral - looking east. The term 'nave' comes from the Latin *navis*, meaning 'ship'. The medieval church thought of itself as a vessel in which the faithful could journey safely to God, and Ely Cathedral is known as the 'Ship of the Fens'.

The design of the Saxon church is unknown, but it is likely to have been a simple rectangular building. When the Normans rebuilt it, they did so in the new cruciform shape, symbolising the Cross on which Jesus died. In the very plan of the church, we are reminded that its life is founded on its faith in Jesus of Nazareth, a faith that sees in him the human face of God, the one who shows us what God is like. The symbolism is continued in the design of the Nave; the ascending sequence of arches, with their repeated three-fold patterning, 'resonates with the Church's belief that God is both one and three, a trinity of persons in a unity of being: God the Father, God the Son, and God the Holy Spirit.'

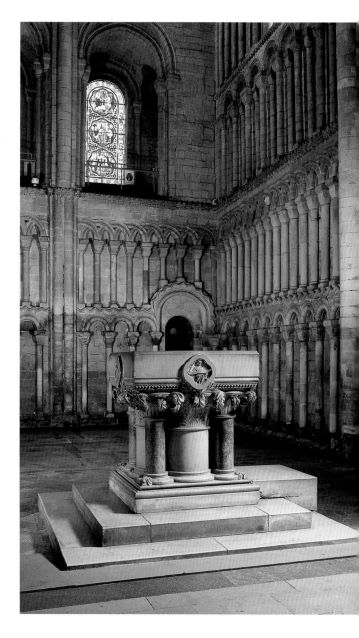

Abbot Simeon began building around 1081, and the work was finished in 1189, many years after his death. Churches were generally built from east to west, and over such a long period architectural styles changed. The style of the nave and transepts is Romanesque, inspired by the Roman buildings of antiquity, and the South-west Transept is one of England's most ornate Romanesque interiors. The arcaded walls grow in complexity as they ascend, and in the topmost tier the transition to an early form of the Gothic style is seen in the pointed arches.

ABOVE: The north side of the Nave showing the three-fold patterning of the design.

RIGHT: The South-west Transept; the font was added in the 19th century.

RIGHT: The West Tower from the Octagon, showing changes in architectural style.

BELOW: The interior of the Galilee Porch, showing the syncopated pattern of the arcade.

The Normans placed the Choir under the central tower and across the Nave a large stone screen, or pulpitum, which separated the people's part of the church from the monks' Choir. The Nave was probably not paved and functioned as a semi-public space in which more secular events might be held. Originally, the West Tower was not as high as it is today; the octagonal top section with its supporting turrets is clearly of a later style and was added in the fourteenth century. On the north side, there was originally a transept to match the one on the south side, with its distinctive 'pepper-pot' turrets. (The North-west Transept was probably taken down in the fifteenth century, following a partial collapse to which the added weight of the octagonal top section may have contributed.) In its original design, before the Galilee Porch was added, the west front was one of the most magnificent of Anglo-Norman church façades.

The term 'Galilee' is often used to describe a building at the west end of a great church. Ely's double-storey Galilee is one of the finest thirteenth-century porches in England. One of its functions was liturgical; after its

tour of the town, the Palm Sunday procession would rest in the Galilee before entering the church, and a boys' choir may have been positioned within the porch on either side, echoing the cries of 'Hosanna!' as the Lord entered his temple. This ancient use has been revived in recent years at Ely.

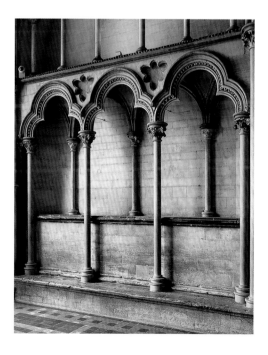

The Monastic Buildings

The Abbey was built with the usual monastic accommodation, including a cloister, chapter house, dormitories, refectory and infirmary. Much of this has been destroyed over the years, but, even so, Ely has the largest collection of medieval monastic buildings in northern Europe still in domestic use. Most of the extant buildings are on the south side, the most notable of which is the Porta, the great gateway into the monastery and adjacent to the monastic barn. Nearby are the Prior's and Abbot's houses, and the Queen's Hall (so named because Queen Philippa stayed there). Firmary Lane marks the site of the monastic infirmary, and on either side four monastic houses were built: to the south are the Black Hostelry (formerly a guest house for Benedictine monks who wore black habits) and Canonry House (now re-named Etheldreda House, where the girl choristers live); and to the north are Walsingham House (where the boy choristers live) and Powcher's Hall, which is named after William Powcher, a former prior.

The range of buildings to the north of the Cathedral housed the sacrist and the almoner, and it was to the Almonry that local people in need came for alms, chiefly in the form of food. The monastery kitchen deliberately produced a considerable surplus so that, in effect, the monks could share their meals with the poor. It now houses the Cathedral restaurant in its atmospheric thirteenth-century undercroft.

The chapter house, cloister and much of the rest of the monastery were destroyed after the Dissolution, with just a small part of the cloister remaining, which is now used as the Song School. Leading off the cloister are two monastic doorways notable for the richness of their decoration. The Monks' Door, which is the entrance to the Cathedral on the south side, has two cusps carved with figures of kneeling priors holding pastoral staffs, and the Prior's Door has a beautiful carved portal, believed to date from c.1120–1140. The tympanum shows Christ enthroned in majesty. His right hand is raised in blessing, and his left hand holds the Book with the Seven Seals, the record of good and

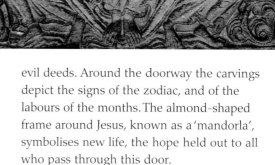

evil deeds. Around the doorway the carvings depict the signs of the zodiac, and of the labours of the months. The almond-shaped frame around Jesus, known as a 'mandorla', symbolises new life, the hope held out to all who pass through this door.

TOP: Firmary Lane and some of the former monastic buildings on the south side of the Cathedral.

ABOVE: The tympanum above the Prior's Door, showing Christ enthroned in Majesty.

INSET: One of the cusps of the Monks' Door with a kneeling prior.

The Cathedral

In 1109 the Abbey became a cathedral. The abbot became the bishop of the new Diocese of Ely, and the prior of the monastery took responsibility for its day-to-day running. One consequence of this was that the Abbey's income was halved, now being split between the monks and the bishop!

The success of Ely as a place of pilgrimage necessitated the remodelling of the area around the shrine in order to provide better accommodation for the pilgrims, and this was the work of Bishop Hugh of Northwold, who rebuilt the east end in the thirteenth century to provide a much larger space for the growing number of pilgrims. The Presbytery, as this part of the church is called (because it is here that the priests, or presbyters, officiate), is in the Early English style. It has a particular gracefulness; the Purbeck marble columns lead the eye up beyond the arches to the rib vault of the ceiling. The quality of the design and workmanship, with its finely proportioned arcade, represents the high point of Early English Gothic. 'There is something immensely satisfying in the way the handsome curves of the great arches, expressed in numerous deeply undercut mouldings, bear down on the glorious foliage capitals.'

ABOVE: Ely Cathedral has the oldest, continuously inhabited set of medieval monastic buildings in the UK.

ABOVE RIGHT: Ceiling boss in the Presbytery, showing St Etheldreda as Abbess of Ely.

LEFT: One of the floriated brackets in the Presbytery, which reflects the miracle of St Etheldreda's sprouting staff. Resting on her flight from Northumberland to Ely, she placed her staff in the ground and the following morning it was found to have budded.

The Presbytery was dedicated in 1252 on the anniversary of the Translation of St Etheldreda, and in the presence of King Henry III and Prince Edward. Her relics were placed in what must have been an imposing elevated sarcophagus, alas destroyed at the Reformation. A simple slate stone slab (left) marks its position today. The setting thus provided for her shrine was nothing short of magnificent, and Bishop Northwold re-dedicated the whole church to her, St Mary and St Peter. The three patron saints are depicted in the ceiling bosses above.

HERE STOOD THE SHRINE OF ETHELDREDA SAINT AND QUEEN WHO FOUNDED THIS HOUSE AD 673

In 1322, only seventy years after the Presbytery was finished, disaster struck. On the night of 12/13 February the square Norman central tower collapsed. It was not entirely unexpected, but nevertheless, when the tower finally fell, the noise and tumult were so great that it was thought there had been an earthquake. The sacrist, Alan of Walsingham, who was responsible for the building, was in deep shock. One of his fellow monks wrote: 'He was devastated, grieving vehemently and overcome with sorrow at an event so disastrous and lamentable that for a moment he knew not which way to turn himself or what to do for the reparation of such a ruin.'

The collapse revealed that the Norman tower was built on unstable ground; so the monks decided to build outwards to find a solid base, and from this evolved the idea of rebuilding the tower as an octagonal space. The span was too wide for this to be done in stone, so instead Alan decided to build a wooden vault from which would rise an octagonal lantern tower over 60 feet (18 metres) high. The Octagon is the Cathedral's crowning glory and it took eighteen years to build. The work was undertaken by master craftsmen under the direction of William Hurley, the king's carpenter. Hurley was widely experienced in undertaking major works in royal palaces and other churches. His achievement was to have been able to scale up the comparatively small cupolas or lanterns that were common in great halls into the altogether larger and grander construction required at Ely.

The decision to rebuild the central tower as an eight-sided structure is unlikely to have been made simply because it fitted the space available. An Octagon is a symbolic shape that points to the Church's belief in the eternal destiny of humankind. Its eight sides stand for the eighth day, the time beyond our earthly time, which we reckon in units of seven days. It reminds us that this is a holy place where we enter the time of eternity. This symbolism is seen also in the decoration, which is conceived from the top downwards. In the centre is Christ in Majesty reigning over all, and around him are the heavenly host, the seraphim and cherubim, with the angels and archangels in the panels below. The decoration descends through the apostles and saints, and the men and women who have been part of Ely's story. Here, where earth and heaven, time and eternity, are joined, the monks sang God's praises and said their prayers. Today the altar where the main Sunday Eucharist is celebrated is situated under the Octagon. In the Eucharist, where the Church remembers the life, death and resurrection of Jesus, heaven is also brought to earth and earth is raised to heaven.

PREVIOUS PAGE: The Presbytery. The two state chairs were used by the Queen and Prince Philip for the Royal Maundy service in 1987.

ABOVE: The Octagon boss showing Christ in Majesty, painted in the fourteenth century by John of Burwell, a village south-east of Ely.

OPPOSITE: The Octagon Altar designed by Luke Hughes.

The Choir and Aisles

The three Norman bays of the Eastern arm of the Cathedral, between the new Octagon and Bishop of Hugh of Northwold's presbytery, were rebuilt in the early fourteenth century at Bishop John Hotham's personal expense, at a cost of nearly 2,035 pounds. The fourteenth-century work is in the Decorated style with a wonderful delicacy in the upper arches. New Choir stalls were constructed and placed in the centre of the Octagon under the lantern where they had previously stood. In the next century the hammer-beam roofs in the transepts, with their flying angels, were installed.

The Choir and Presbytery are the heart of the Cathedral. The aisle that surrounds them is used for burials and memorials, and around one hundred people from Ely's history are buried or remembered here, from Bishop Hugh Northwold (who died in the thirteenth century) to Canon Dennis Green (who died at the end of the twentieth century). Many of the monuments that are now placed against the external walls were originally placed against the columns on the inner side. Today, when special permission has to be obtained in order to make any internal alterations to the Cathedral, the freedom with which our predecessors moved around the memorials and other features is quite extraordinary.

ABOVE: The arches of the Choir Triforium.

BELOW: One of the flying angels in the hammer-beam roof of the South Transept.

OPPOSITE: The Choir and Presbytery from the Octagon. In the arch a medieval painting of the Crucifixion can be seen.

14

At the eastern end of each aisle is a chantry chapel. The fear of divine punishment was very real in the Middle Ages, and chantries were endowed to pay for a priest to say Mass for the souls of the founder and his friends to lessen their time in purgatory. (The chantry priests often held another appointment as a schoolmaster or chaplain. When the chantries were suppressed in 1547, it is said it caused a great loss to education in England.) John Alcock, who founded the chapel on the north side, became Bishop of Ely in 1486. Like many bishops of his day, he was a servant of both Church and State; he founded Jesus College, Cambridge, and held the office of Lord Chancellor. His chapel has a beautiful fan-vault ceiling, the only one in Ely.

On the south side is Bishop West's Chantry Chapel with a fine coffered ceiling – probably the last decorative work in the Cathedral before the Dissolution. Nicholas West was a brilliant diplomat; his great moment came when he managed to seal a defensive alliance with France by persuading François I to pay a debt of one million crowns owed by his predecessor to Henry VIII. Cardinal Wolsey saw that West was rewarded for his work, and he became Bishop of Ely in 1515. Although he lived in great style, employing over one hundred servants, it is said that he provided cooked food for over two hundred poor people every day.

Walking down the South Choir Aisle is to walk through the changes in Christian belief and artistic style over five centuries. At the east end is the large memorial to John Tiptoft (d.1443), who lies between his two wives in a pious pose typical of the Age of Chivalry; while opposite is Bishop Peter Gunning (d.1684), who reclines and gestures in the mannered style of the Baroque period.

RIGHT: The South Choir Aisle with Bishop West's Chantry Chapel at the far end. Statues once stood in the now empty niches on the façade, but they were destroyed in the Reformation.

INSET: The ceiling in Bishop Alcock's Chapel.

LEFT: The baroque memorial to Bishop Peter Gunning, bishop from 1675 to 1684.

ABOVE: The medieval memorial to John Tiptoft, (c.1378–1443) who rests between his two wives.

Further along is the memorial to Bishop Thomas Green (d.1738), which is notable for the absence of any Christian imagery; instead, it has the classical funerary urns and sombre drapes typical of the Age of Reason. At the west end of the aisle the Victorian bishop, Joseph Allen (d.1845), reclines on a couch in the manner of a Roman dinner guest. By contrast, the more modern memorials tend to be simple inscriptions.

LEFT: The Victorian memorial to Bishop Joseph Allen, bishop from 1836 to 1845.

The Lady Chapel

The thirteenth and fourteenth centuries were notable for the rise of the cult of the Virgin Mary, especially in England, and Lady chapels in her honour were added to many churches. There was already a small Lady Chapel in Ely, in what is now the South Choir Aisle, and the *piscina* in which the sacred vessels were cleansed can still be seen. But the chapel was not large enough, so a new one was built on the north side of the Presbytery. The Lady Chapel of Ely, the largest attached to any British cathedral, is exceptional. Its construction was overseen by one of the monks, John of Wisbech, who died in the Black Death. It was built at the same time as the Octagon, and was completed in 1349, having taken twenty-eight years to build. It is notable for the richness of its decoration, particularly that of the wall arcade, at the time the most elaborate to have been built in Europe. Over each of the double seats of the arcade, supported by buttresses of Alwalton marble, are arches with three-dimensional double curves known as 'nodding ogees': 'everything in this design is in movement and every surface is carved in minute detail.'

When completed, the chapel looked very different to how it is today. It was highly coloured, the windows were alive with stained glass and there were painted statues in the niches – the remains of this medieval colouring can still be seen. All this was destroyed in the Reformation and the damage is heartbreaking: the windows are now plain glass, all the exquisite figures in the lower niches have been defaced, and above are the empty pedestals where the statues once stood. The chapel is an eloquent reminder of the power of religious ideas and the way that they can be used destructively. The death of Jesus was the result of the same forces at work, and his body, broken on the Cross, bears the pain of the brokenness of the world.

The frieze carvings show the story of Mary's life and miracles. The main sources for the stories of Mary are two texts that captured the popular imagination in the Middle Ages: the apocryphal *Gospel of Pseudo-Matthew*, which claimed to fill in some of the missing details of the early life of Mary and Jesus; and *The Golden Legend*, a collection of stories about the saints including the Dormition (or death) of Mary, her Assumption into heaven and the miracles ascribed to her prayers.

OPPOSITE: The Lady Chapel before the installation in 2011 of the reredos and altar designed by John Maddison.

BELOW: The Lady Chapel arcade, showing the nodding ogees and the damaged figures of the frieze carving.

Dissolution and Reform

The pilgrims who came to worship at St Etheldreda's shrine contributed to the growing wealth of the monastery. Along with Glastonbury and Winchester, Ely became one of the three wealthiest monasteries in England – but with wealth came corruption. The Benedictine Order had substantially lost sight of its ideals, its vigour was spent and its numbers were in serious decline. Reform was long overdue and, when it came, it unleashed a tide of destruction. As the monasteries were dissolved, so were their treasures confiscated, the statues and the images defaced, the windows smashed and the shrine of St Etheldreda destroyed. All this destruction was decreed by the then Bishop of Ely, Thomas Goodrich: 'All images, relics, memorials, shrines, etcetera, shall be so totally demolished and obliterated with all speed and diligence that no remains or memory of them might be found for the future.' The Bishop's men did their work thoroughly and virtually nothing remains of Ely's medieval decoration. It is ironic that Goodrich's tomb is one of the few with its memorial brass more or less intact, and roped off to protect it from damage!

Ely became one of the cathedrals of King Henry VIII's 'New Foundation', as did the other former monastic churches that were also cathedrals, and its dedication was changed to 'The Cathedral Church of the Holy and Undivided Trinity'. The prior and the monks were replaced by a dean, eight canons and six minor canons. The King also established a school for boys to sing the services – the beginning of the King's School in Ely, where the present choristers are also educated.

Just over one hundred years after the Dissolution of the Monasteries, Oliver Cromwell became Governor of the Isle of Ely. The Puritans rejected all but the plainest forms of worship – in a letter to the Precentor, Cromwell described the choir service as 'so unedifying and offensive'– and during the Commonwealth, Ely ceased to function as a cathedral (though occasional services were held), the only time in its history when it has not been open for worship every day. It seems likely, however, that Cromwell's intervention spared Ely from the more violent actions of the Reformers. The chapter house and the cloisters were demolished, and there was even a plan to take down the whole building so that its materials might be sold to the benefit of 'sick and maimed soldiers, widows and orphans'. Although the Reformation damage was serious, when Celia Fiennes recorded her visit to Ely in 1698, she could remark, 'this church has the most popish remains in its walls as any I have seen'.

RIGHT: The memorial brass of Bishop Thomas Goodrich in the South Choir Aisle. He was bishop from 1534 to 1555.

Beginning Again

The restoration of the monarchy in 1660 brought a complete change of policy. The choir services were reinstituted and money was raised for the refurbishment of the Choir, and for repairs to the church. As the seventeenth century came to a close, on 29 March 1699, the north-west corner of the North Transept collapsed. The Chapter decided that it should be rebuilt 'exactly in the manner and on the same foundations as it stood before'. Given the general lack of interest in ancient buildings at the time, this decision was quite remarkable and required the careful copying of all the Romanesque detail as well as the Gothic windows.

The eighteenth century saw changes within the building, overseen by the architect James Essex. He repaired and remodelled the Octagon; this included, among other things, the removal of the flying buttresses, and he constructed a new roof over the Choir and Presbytery. He took down the pulpitum across the Nave; removed the Choir stalls to the east end; placed the high altar directly under the east window; and built a new organ screen across the western end of the Choir.

ABOVE: The boy choristers at Evensong.

INSET: Roof boss in the Presbytery, showing the Coronation of the Blessed Virgin Mary.

Essex's work notwithstanding, by the end of the eighteenth century the Cathedral was in a parlous state. William Cobbett, who visited Ely on 28 March 1813, was appalled at what he saw: 'This famous building, the cathedral, is in a state of disgraceful irrepair and disfigurement.' The architect and chief protagonist of the Gothic revival in England, A. W. N. Pugin, on walking into the Lady Chapel and seeing it cluttered with cheap box pews and covered in thick coats of lime wash, is said to have burst into tears exclaiming, 'O God, what has England done to deserve this.' Things changed with the appointment in 1839 of a new dean: George Peacock, Lowndean Professor of Astronomy and Geometry at Cambridge. The early

LEFT: The portrait of Dean Peacock by D. W. Blakiston (1860), which hangs in the North Choir aisle, above the memorial to Dean Henry Caesar. It was discovered in the vaults of Barclays Bank in Norwich, and returned to the Cathedral in 1989.

Victorian period saw a reawakening in the importance of cathedral and church architecture, and when Peacock arrived at Ely he found a group of canons enthusiastic for the work of restoration. One of these was Edward Bowyer Sparke, the son of a former bishop, and it was largely due to his personal generosity, and that of his family, that much of the restoration work was made possible. Dean Peacock and the canons set about a major restoration with characteristic Victorian energy and zeal. They were initially advised by Robert Willis – who has been described as the father of cathedral archaeology – and later by George Gilbert Scott, who had been much influenced by Pugin.

LEFT: St Catherine's Chapel in the South-west Transept. The Chapel was rebuilt in 1849–50 after careful study of the ruined remains and the surrounding architecture.

OPPOSITE: Two of the paired carved panels in the canopies above the Choir stalls, showing Noah's Ark, *top*, and the Baptism of Jesus, *below*.

The first task was to restore the South-west Transept. For some time it had been used as a workshop with a screen separating it from the rest of the building. The screen was removed and the great arch reopened. St Catherine's Chapel was rebuilt, and the contrast between the medieval and the Victorian work is clearly visible. A new font was installed in the South-west Transept, which became the baptistery, and a new pavement was laid, the area beneath the tower, just inside the West door, depicting a labyrinth. Walking a labyrinth is an ancient spiritual exercise; its twists and turns mirror the path of life, as we move towards the centre, our heavenly destiny. Fonts are usually sited at the threshold of a church, because it is through baptism, the ceremony performed at the font, that we become members of the Church and set out on a new path of life.

James Essex's organ screen was demolished and the Choir stalls were moved to their present position. A new Choir screen was built with towering pinnacles typical of Scott's work. Its open design enabled those seated in the Nave to hear and see the Choir service, and this screen set the pattern for new choir screens up and down the land. The contractor for the whole project was James Rattee, whose firm was based in Cambridge and was associated with the restoration of the Cathedral right up to the end of the twentieth century.

To the medieval Choir stalls Scott added the sub-stalls in front and a series of carved panels in the canopies above. These are the work of Michel Abeloos of Louvain in Belgium, who also carved the figures on the Choir screen. On the south side the scenes are from the Old Testament, with corresponding scenes from the New Testament on the north side; for example, the Creation of Adam is paired with the Birth of Jesus, and his Baptism with the Flood.

Removing the organ screen caused the organ to be relocated to the North Choir Triforium. The decorative organ case, with its profusion of angels, was inspired by the one in Strasbourg Cathedral. At the same time the roofs were repaired, heating was installed and the floors were partially repaved.

In 1850 work began on the reredos, which took eighteen years to complete at a cost of £4,000. It was given by John Dunne Gardner of Chatteris as a memorial to his first wife. Designed by George Gilbert Scott in the Italian style, it has the same exuberance and richness as the Choir screen, and restores some of the colour lost at the Reformation. Its five panels show the events of Holy Week, from Jesus' entry into Jerusalem on Palm Sunday to his walk to

Golgotha on Good Friday. Holy Week is the most important week of the Christian Year, when the Church celebrates the central mystery of the Christian faith, the sacrificial death of the Son of God. A series of special services solemnly recall the trial, suffering and death of Jesus, and his joyful Resurrection on Easter Day. Jesus taught that God is love and his self-giving, to the point of self-sacrifice on the Cross, shows the depth of the love of God for the world.

ABOVE: The central panel of the reredos, showing Jesus and the disciples at the Last Supper, recalled in the Eucharist celebrated each week at the altar.

BELOW: The ornate organ case by George Gilbert Scott, which is decorated with 24 angels playing trumpets.

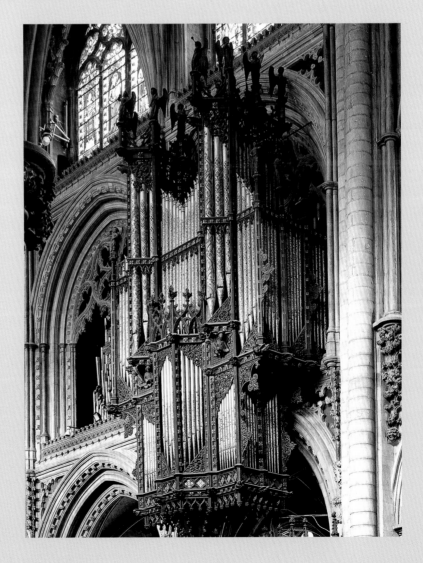

ABOVE: George Gilbert Scott's reredos in the Italian style. The five panels show the events of Holy Week: from the left, the Entry into Jerusalem, the Washing of the Feet, the Last Supper, the Agony in the Garden of Gethsemane, and Jesus carrying the Cross.

The Nave Ceiling

The next project was to construct the remarkable painted ceiling in the Nave. The medieval rafters were covered with planks and were painted by two Victorian artists who did it as a labour of love. Henry Styleman le Strange painted the first six panels but then sadly died, and his friend Thomas Gambier Parry painted the last six. Parry said of his work in the Nave: 'It was a very awkward work to execute, lying on one's back, in a painfully bad light, impeded by the scaffolding and without the possibility of getting a clear view of it at a fair distance, to judge of it in various stages of its progress.' The ceiling tells the story of the ancestry of Jesus, beginning with Adam and continuing through Abraham, Jacob and David. The last four panels have New Testament themes: the Annunciation, the Nativity, the Adoration of the Magi and Christ in Majesty. The roundels around the edge depict the ancestors of Jesus as given by St Luke in his Gospel. It was completed in time for Christmas, 1864.

Finally, beginning in 1859, the Octagon was repaired and restored. The intention was to create a 'broadly reliable reconstruction of William Hurley's masterpiece' in memory of Dean Peacock who had died in the previous year. Appropriately, the windows in the lantern show the initials 'GP' alternating with a peacock motif. Thomas Gambier Parry painted the vault underneath the Octagon, and the angel panels as an illustration of psalm 150: 'O praise God in his holiness; praise him in the firmament of his power.'

ABOVE: The central panels of the Nave ceiling showing the different styles of the two artists. In the top panel Parry uses stronger colours and richer compositions; his supporting figures extend over the borders, unlike Le Strange (lower panel) who left them freestanding.

RIGHT: Eight of the 32 angels in the panels around the base of the Octagon lantern. Parry painted them playing instruments in use in the 14th century, when the Octagon was built.

OPPOSITE: The 12 panels of the Nave ceiling.

The Stained Glass

The Victorian period also saw the reglazing of the windows, and Ely illustrates better than any other building the Victorian revival in stained glass. There are more than one hundred windows by most of the significant glass painters of the period. The windows illustrate the main stories of the Bible with Old Testament themes in the Nave, and New Testament themes around the Presbytery. Church windows are really teaching aids, an ever-present reminder that the Christian faith is based on real events in the lives of real people. The series reaches its climax with the story of Jesus' life in the East Window – a life that was so significant that the calendar was stopped and restarted from the date of his birth. It is the work of William Wailes and its medieval style was inspired by the windows of Chartres and Bourges. It was paid for by a large legacy from Bishop Sparke. The south lancet shows the Annunciation and the stories of Jesus' birth; the north lancet, his ministry and miracles; and the centre lancet, his Passion: the entry into Jerusalem, arrest, trial and crucifixion. The window above shows the Resurrection, the Ascension and Christ in Majesty. Here the Christian story is told simply and beautifully, and the window is often used by pilgrims and visitors as a source of meditation.

In the late 1850s the firm of Clayton & Bell came to prominence as a dominant force in glass painting, and Ely has some excellent work by them, in particular a series of windows in the South Choir Aisle (paid for by the Sparke family), which illustrate scenes from the Gospels. They show 'a clarity of design and colour which represents high Victorian art at its most appealing and decorative'. There are also windows representing later styles, for example, Henry Holiday's pre-Raphaelite depiction of Christ Healing the Sick (in the South Choir Aisle), and Sir Ninian Comper's window depicting a rather youthful Christ in Majesty in Bishop West's Chapel.

The Cathedral is also home to the National Stained Glass Museum, situated in the South Nave Triforium, the only museum in England to concentrate exclusively on stained glass. On display are over one hundred panels, including medieval glass from France and England, and more modern works by William Morris and John Piper. The collection includes a portrait of King George III (1793) by James Pearson, loaned by Her Majesty the Queen, and a very striking depiction of St Wilfrid and St John Berchmans (1927) by Harry Clark, from the Lady Chapel of the Convent Notre Dame, Dowanhill, Glasgow.

Pride of place is given to a beautiful medieval window from Soissons Cathedral (*c.*1210), which shows the bust of a king by an anonymous artist; it was acquired in 2003. The museum also has an extensive reserve collection and an attractive gift shop selling original works. A booklet about the stained glass of Ely Cathedral is available from the Cathedral Shop.

OPPOSITE: The Choir screen by George Gilbert Scott, which served as a model for similar screens throughout the land.

TOP: Detail from the East Window, showing the donor Bishop Sparke at prayer.

ABOVE: The window from Soissons Cathedral in the Stained Glass Museum.

ABOVE: The window in Bishop West's Chapel by Ninian Comper (1947), showing Christ in Majesty with St Basil and St John Chrysostom.

ABOVE: Jesus Walking on Water by Clayton & Bell (1860).

RIGHT: Jesus Healing the Sick by Henry Holliday (1893).

ABOVE: The Tower of Babel by John G Howe (1850).

OPPOSITE: Two roundels from the East Window by William Wailes (1857), showing the Baptism of Jesus and his Temptation by the Devil.

The Twentieth Century

The early years of the new century saw the rebuilding of the organ by Harrison & Harrison in 1908. It was their first major job and established their reputation as organ builders, and it was the prototype for their cathedral organ style. With four manuals and 5,606 pipes, it is a magnificent instrument and was completely renovated in 2000.

The two world wars of the twentieth century left their mark on the Cathedral. After World War I, St George's Chapel was dedicated as the memorial to those of the Cambridgeshire Regiment who had died, and the panels contain 864 names. A Memorial Book contains a further 784 names of those who died in World War II. St Etheldreda's Chapel was reordered as a memorial to all those from Cambridgeshire and the Isle of Ely who gave their lives. This chapel also includes a fine statue of St Etheldreda by Philip Turner, made in 1961. In the North Choir Aisle a new window was donated by Bomber Command of the New Zealand Air Force as a memorial to their servicemen and to those of the RAF, who had flown out of airfields near Ely.

In 1958 the Chapel of St Dunstan and St Ethelwold was created by converting the southern bay of the Chapter Library.

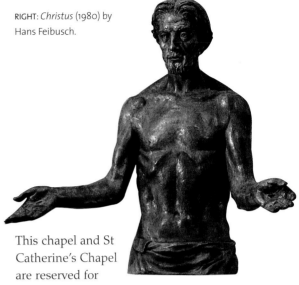

This chapel and St Catherine's Chapel are reserved for private prayer. In 1964 David Wynne's *Noli me tangere* was installed in the South Transept. The movement of the sculpture is in the arms of the figures, and their thinness is designed to focus attention – in this case, on the moving encounter between Jesus and Mary Magdalene on the first Easter Day. As Mary reaches out to Jesus he says to her, 'Do not cling to me, for I have not yet ascended to the Father. But go to my brothers, and tell them that I am ascending to my Father and your Father, to my God and your God.' (John 20.17) In 1980 another sculpture, Hans Feibusch's fine bronze *Christus*, was acquired and placed to welcome visitors at the West Door.

The Great Restoration

The final fourteen years of the twentieth century saw another major programme of restoration overseen by two deans, William Patterson and Michael Higgins, who worked with the architects Peter Miller and Jane Kennedy. In 1986 the lead on the Nave roof was damaged in severe winds, and inspection revealed serious deterioration in other parts of the building. Over the following years, the Great Restoration (as it came to be called) saw the repair of the roofs and the systematic repair and restoration of the stonework, both inside and outside. The Nave ceiling was cleaned, the windows of the Octagon lantern were repaired and strengthened, and in 1994 the Prior's Door was enclosed. Most notably, the Processional Way was constructed, restoring the medieval passageway used by pilgrims to move from St Etheldreda's shrine to the Lady Chapel. Designed by Jane Kennedy, it was the first substantial addition to the building since the Middle Ages.

The windows were designed by Helen Whittaker and made by Keith Barley of York. The five roof bosses are by Peter Ball, one of which is shown in the inset. Finally, a new floor was laid in the Lady Chapel, also designed by Jane Kennedy, which won an award in 2004 for the best stone interior. Rebuilding the North-west transept was also contemplated, but the estimated cost was £45 million, which put an end to the dream – at least for the time being! The cost of the whole campaign was £12 million subscribed by private donations, partly through the newly founded Order of St Etheldreda, and supplemented by funds from English Heritage. The Cathedral is now in the best state of repair that it has ever been.

BELOW: One of the Octagon buttresses, showing the renewed lead work carried out as part of the Great Restoration.

RIGHT: The Processional Way. The memorial stone records the re-interment of 24 persons from the wider monastic community, discovered during the building works.

THIS PROCESSION WAY STANDS ON FOUNDATIONS OF THE [...] USED BY PILGRIMS TO [...] RECENT HISTORY [...] SOCIAL [...] IT WAS REMADE [...] REMEMBERING [...] INTRODUCING DURING BUILDING WORK AD 2000

The Millennium Sculptures

To mark the third millennium, three new sculptures were commissioned and installed in the year 2000. Adjacent to the labyrinth, and complementing its symbolism, is Jonathan Clarke's *The Way of Life*. It is in cast aluminium with nine sections, each differently jointed. Like the journey of life, its path is irregular and unpredictable; and as the journey is sometimes hard, sometimes joyful, so the surface texture and the colour also vary. Perhaps to give a human scale to the journey, Jonathan Clarke placed a tiny human figure on the top arm of the cross.

Over the pulpit is Peter Ball's *Christ in Glory*, a modern rendering of the same theme as the central boss of the Octagon ceiling. It is made from driftwood, like much of Ball's work. In the Lady Chapel a new statue of Mary by David Wynne was installed above the altar. It is carved from Portland stone and weighs half a ton. Most representations of Mary are passive; Wynne shows her as expressive, exulting in the news that she is to be the mother of the Saviour. The inscription on the base is a quotation from St Luke's Gospel: 'Behold the handmaiden of the Lord.'

ABOVE: *Christ in Glory* (2000) by Peter Ball, above the pulpit.

LEFT: *The Blessed Virgin Mary* (2000) by David Wynne, in the Lady Chapel.

OPPOSITE: *The Way of Life* (2000) by Jonathan Clarke, underneath the West Tower.

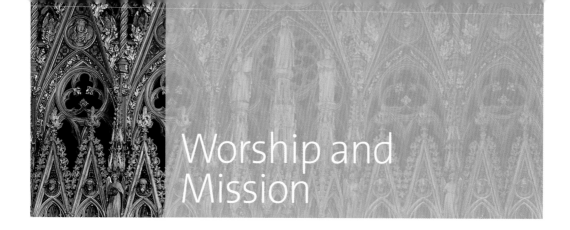

Worship and Mission

The closing decades of the twentieth century saw a profound change in the life of the English cathedrals. This was the result of the new spirit of renewal at work in the worldwide Church, which coincided with a growing number of visitors and the growth of the heritage movement. People of all faiths and none began to value cathedrals as places where they could experience quiet and stillness, in contrast to the bustle of modern life, and could lose themselves in the beautiful music that characterises cathedral worship. Over the centuries, Ely has been served by a number of distinguished musicians, among them John Amner, Tertius Noble, Basil Harwood and Arthur Wills.

The daily round of worship, inherited from its Benedictine past, is the heartbeat of the Cathedral. At the start of the day, Morning Prayer is said and the Eucharist celebrated, with each of the chapels being used in turn during the course of a week. At the end of the day, Evening Prayer is sung in the Choir.

ABOVE: A priest breaks the bread in the Eucharist, the heart of the daily worship of the Cathedral.

ABOVE: Choral Evensong. The choir comprises up to 22 boys and six lay clerks, rising to 12 on Sundays and major festivals.

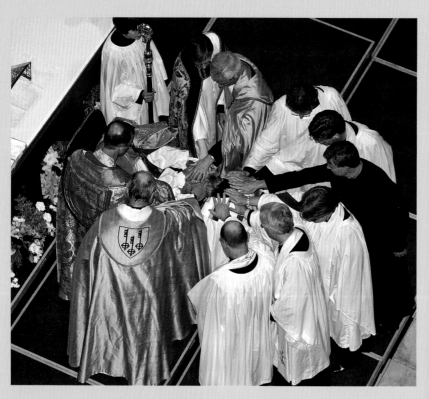

ABOVE: A priest is ordained by the Bishop of Ely and assisting clergy, at the annual Ordination of Deacons and Priests.

ABOVE: The Amnesty candle burns continuously on the altar of Bishop Alcock's Chantry Chapel, which is set aside for prayer for prisoners of conscience. The reredos by John Maddison was installed in 2004 and shows the instruments of the Passion.

LEFT: The Ely Cathedral Girls Choir.

BELOW: The Ely Imps rehearsing with Paul Trepte, the Director of Music.

This is the *Opus Dei*, the work of God, and it has been performed at Ely for over thirteen centuries since St Etheldreda founded her church, with the sole exception of the period when the Cathedral was closed during the Commonwealth. In addition to the daily round of services, the Cathedral is used for major diocesan services such as the annual Ordination of Deacons and Priests, and for services celebrating important national and civic occasions.

Over the centuries since King Henry VIII founded the choir, the services have been sung by a traditional choir of men and boys until, in 2006, the Ely Cathedral Girls Choir, founded by the King's School, Ely, was formed. The Cathedral also supports a large voluntary choir, the Ely Cathedral Octagon Singers, and a children's choir, The Ely Imps, who sing on special occasions. The Imps are part of the Ely Singing Project, a government-sponsored scheme that seeks to utilise the musical resources of cathedrals to promote singing in schools.

Education and Outreach

Perhaps the most noticeable effect of the changing role of the Cathedral has been in the expansion of its educational work. The Benedictine monastery at Ely was an important place of learning, and today that work continues. Around eight thousand school children visit the Cathedral each year, and take part in activities that cannot be undertaken in the classroom. They can experience a day in the life of a Benedictine monk, or dress as a medieval pilgrim and take a gift to St Etheldreda's shrine. They search for animals in the windows or find monsters in the misericords; they wonder at the Octagon and hear the story of its building; they measure the pillars and create their own labyrinths; they reflect on the *Way of Life*. The aim is to let the building tell its story in ways that resonate with the stories of the children.

The Cathedral also offers an adult education programme, including the annual St Etheldreda Lecture, in honour of the Cathedral's foundress, which is given by a woman whose life's work has made a difference in Church or State. Courses and weekend seminars focus on the history and heritage of Ely, including the Benedictine tradition, relating St Benedict's teaching on community and leadership to issues in contemporary life and work. There are also regular discipleship courses for those seeking baptism or confirmation, or for those who simply wish to deepen their understanding of the Christian faith. Less formal education takes place through exhibitions, art, poetry evenings, *Son et Lumière* presentations and pilgrimage tours to enable the wider public to engage with issues of faith and morality from a Christian perspective.

Through its links with Zanzibar Cathedral, with Schleswig (Germany) and with Hackney (London), the Cathedral encourages a two-way process of learning, discovery and mutual support by engaging with issues of wealth, poverty, justice, ecumenism and inter-faith dialogue. Through the link, members of the Cathedral support around thirty children from Zanzibar whose families are too poor to pay for secondary education. The Cathedral also provides an important venue for concerts and exhibitions.

TOP: The annual 'Rave in the Nave' attracts a thousand young people from a wide-reaching area, well beyond Ely, for an evening of contemporary Christian music, activities, reflection and worship.

RIGHT: Several times a year, the Cathedral is filled with children for the annual series of Schools' Days.

OPPOSITE: The West Tower looking up: in the centre of the ceiling is one of many representations of Christ in Majesty in the Cathedral. The *Way of Life* sculpture is on the right.

PREVIOUS PAGE: Winter frost on the Nave and West Tower heralds the onset of Christmas.

A Holy Place

The Cathedral is not just an awe-inspiring building but a holy place where the ordinary is transcended. Over the centuries, the daily round of prayer, music and sacrament has given the Cathedral its particular character and atmosphere. It is as though the very stones have soaked up the devotion of the ages. When it was built, Ely was just a small settlement. Out of the way places were often chosen for monasteries; the monks sought space for the spirit away from the distractions of the world. Today many people, whatever they believe, sense the absence of the spiritual dimension in modern life, and the Cathedral offers to all who come, space for the spirit and an invitation to look again at the faith that inspired those who built it.

The invitation has changed over the centuries. This is shown in the way in which the most common theme in the decoration of the Cathedral, Christ in Majesty, has changed. Above the labyrinth and the Prior's Door, in the Nave ceiling and the Octagon boss, in the East Window and elsewhere, Jesus is shown somewhat sternly as Judge of all the world. By contrast, Peter Ball's sculpture above the pulpit shows a much more benign countenance. Its title, *Christ in Glory*, reflects the fact that judgment does not speak to people today as it did in former times; rather, we seek a faith that will give us a glimpse of glory and meaning to our lives.

Jonathan Clarke's *Way of Life* makes the same point. His sculpture has no iconic meaning; its symbolism is open, leaving the pilgrim to project his or her own meaning on to it, just as walking the labyrinth encourages a personal reflection on the meaning and pattern of one's life. In the modern works we do not see the judgmental proclamation of the medieval Church but a more humble invitation to explore the way to God.

From its foundation until the dissolution of the monastery, the work of the Cathedral was inspired by the Benedictine spirit of hospitality. St Benedict said that visitors to the monastery should be welcomed like Christ, and today the Cathedral is seeking to learn from its Benedictine heritage by offering a welcome to all who come, whether as pilgrims or as tourists, to pray and learn, or just to look. As its beauty and grandeur speak of the majesty, the love and the peace of God, so its people – congregation, staff and volunteers – strive to be, in the words of its mission statement, a Christian community of worship, welcome and care.

LEFT: Visitors are welcomed to the Cathedral.

OPPOSITE: The Octagon ceiling with Christ in Majesty in the central boss.